Cyber Essentials

A Pocket Guide

Cyber Essentials

A Pocket Guide

ALAN CALDER

IT Governance Publishing

IT Governance Publishing
IT Governance Limited
Unit 3, Clive Court
Bartholomew's Walk
Ely, Cambridgeshire
CB7 4EA, United Kingdom

www.itgovernance.co.uk

© Alan Calder 2014

The author has asserted the rights of the author under the Copyright, Designs and Patents Act, 1988, to be identified as the author of this work.

First published in the United Kingdom in 2014 by IT Governance Publishing.

ISBN 978-1-84928-688-6

CONTENTS

INTRODUCTION

The origins of the Cyber Essentials scheme

Thousands of IT systems are compromised every day – a shocking fact. But when you consider the proliferation of cyber threats in recent years, it isn't surprising that some of them are successful. Although cyber activists and spies often get more press, most are carried out by criminals and fraudsters looking for financial gain. The most common kinds of attacks now require little skill or expertise to carry out, and use technology which is widely available online – according to the Verizon 2013 Data Breach Investigations Report, 78% of the attacks they monitor fall into this category.

The UK Government wants to be sure that partners and contractors have a basic level of security in place to protect the data stored in their systems against these low-tech cyber attacks. The Government became aware that certification to a cyber security standard was often beyond the capability of small and medium-sized organisations (SMEs) and established the Cyber Essentials scheme in response. It is based on the advice given in the earlier publications *10 Steps to Cyber Security* and *Small Businesses: What you need to know about cyber security*.

From 1 October 2014 all suppliers bidding for a range of government ICT contracts – in particular contracts requiring the handling of sensitive and personal information – must be certified to the scheme. Furthermore, suppliers will have to be reassessed at least once a year. Organisations can be certified to either Cyber Essentials or Cyber Essentials Plus (level 2 of the scheme), which demonstrates an even greater commitment to cyber security but requires an additional investment of money and organisational effort.

Why get certified?

You are probably reading this guide because UK Government contracts can be very lucrative and your company is therefore willing to deal with a lot of frustrating red tape to get one. Cyber Essentials should not be seen as a bureaucratic hold-up to business, however. The Information Assurance for Small and Medium Enterprises Consortium (IASME), the Information Security Forum (ISF) and the British Standards Institution (BSI) have all been deeply involved in the creation of the scheme, with the result that you can meet the requirements using easy to implement, low-cost solutions.

In today's climate the business case for certification to a scheme like this goes beyond obtaining government contracts. For a start, take a look at the results of IT Governance's international 2014 Boardroom Cyber Watch Survey. We asked whether respondents had received a customer query about their company's information security credentials during the previous 12 months, and 55% of the 240 respondents said yes, a 5% increase on the previous year's survey. It is clear that cyber security is of increasing importance to private companies as well as governments.

There is also a good chance that your organisation is already compliant with many of the controls, so becoming certified is not only valuable but often quite easy.

This is no reason for complacency, however; even large organisations may not have covered every control. To ensure that your ability to bid for a contract is not undermined, to protect from future legal consequences and to make sure that you only have to go through the auditing process once, it is crucial that you ensure you are fully compliant with the entire *Assurance Framework*; this book should help you to achieve that goal.

What am I protecting?

Low-level cyber attacks are usually targeted against the most vulnerable elements of your IT infrastructure. Any hardware which can be connected to the Internet can also be compromised, including desktop computers, laptops, smartphones, tablets and servers.

Sometimes computers are hijacked so that they can be used to perform attacks on others (e.g. denial-of-service attacks), to remotely send out spam or to store illegal materials. The aim of most cyber attackers, however, is to steal data such as sensitive business information or financial records. The personal details of staff and customers are a common target, and if you have access to data that can be used for the purposes of fraud (such as cardholder data and sensitive authentication data) your organisation will be of particular interest to online criminals.

With the increase in cyber attacks on SMEs (87% were hit in 2012, up 10% from the year before according to the Department for Business, Innovation and Skills), all of the security measures required by Cyber Essentials are also general good practice which should be put in place by all such enterprises. Failure to take cyber security seriously can result in theft, fraud, damage to reputation and even legal repercussions – in other words, by putting these controls in place you are defending critical areas of your business. You are also protecting your reputation – it is highly embarrassing to publicly admit that you have been the victim of a low-tech cyber attack because it shows to all your customers that their information is not being adequately protected.

Beyond and outside Cyber Essentials

It is worth noting that the scheme only lays out the UK Government's minimum acceptable security standards, which ensure a basic level of protection against prevalent threats and reduce vulnerability to breaches. As such, the controls discussed here are just the starting point for companies which are serious about protecting themselves and their customers. Organisations facing more advanced opposition, especially targeted attacks, should create a stronger security apparatus – fortunately the security requirements laid out by Cyber Essentials are in line with well established standards such as ISO/IEC 27001 or the Information Security Forum's *Standard of Good Practice for Information Security*, and can therefore form the central component of a more comprehensive security infrastructure in the future.

Note that due to the fact that it has been designed to cover only the most common software and hardware systems in use, certain varieties of software cannot be certified as secure under Cyber Essentials – for example, Point of Sales (POS) software, Pin Entry Devices (PED) and eCommerce applications. These systems have different vulnerabilities and therefore require some different kinds of protection on top of the basic rules outlined in the scheme.

Structure of the book

The Cyber Essentials scheme consists of three documents:

1. *Cyber Essentials Scheme: Summary* gives an overview of the entire scheme, including the scope, structure, key controls and levels of certification. It also includes a FAQ.

2. *Cyber Essentials Scheme: Requirements for basic technical protection from cyber attacks* lays out the technical requirements necessary to achieve compliance with the scheme (known as 'controls').

3. *Cyber Essentials Scheme: Assurance Framework* explains the independent assurance process for both the assessor and the company being assessed, covering both Cyber Essentials and Cyber Essentials Plus. It also discusses the scoping process.

The documents are available from the UK Government at this website: *www.gov.uk/ government/publications/cyber-essentials-scheme-overview*.

This book will first examine the *Requirements* in detail: discussing the controls, explaining why they are necessary and suggesting ways to put them in place so that certification is likely at the end of the implementation process.

Secondly we will look at the *Assurance Framework*: examining the first step in becoming compliant (scoping), helping you to determine whether you are ready to undergo assessment and presenting an analysis of how the certification process works.

The final part of the book presents a selection of additional resources that are available to help you implement the controls: it includes further reading and consultancy options, and also covers some sensible steps your organisation can make if you would like to take cyber security beyond the basic level mandated in Cyber Essentials.

PART I: REQUIREMENTS FOR BASIC TECHNICAL PROTECTION FROM CYBER ATTACKS

The controls set out in the *Requirements* are relevant to organisations of all sizes, but have been chosen for Cyber Essentials because they are relatively easy to implement for SMEs and protect against a wide variety of common cyber threats. But what are the common attacks that your organisation faces, and which the UK Government are so keen to protect against?

Types of attack

The image of the hacker in popular media is usually of a lone individual in a basement, tapping away at a keyboard, trying to break into a specific computer system. This targeted attack methodology is not how most attackers operate, which is lucky because it is difficult to keep out a motivated and expert cyber criminal who is deliberately targeting your organisation.

The good news is that most cyber attackers run their criminal enterprises like a business, and it is just not economical for them to go after their targets one-by-one. Successful cyber attacks in the UK generally rely on simple technology that is widely available on the web. Such attackers employ a scattergun approach, using vectors such as spam email to go after hundreds of organisations and individuals at once, and then opportunistically break into exposed networks – these are known as 'commodity' cyber threats. To break into a system, the attackers rely on poor technical security measures at target organisations and/or a lack of security awareness among staff – so addressing these issues goes a long way toward making your organisation secure.

The types of common attack can be split into five major categories:

1. Social engineering
   Attackers 'con' employees into allowing them to access the organisation's systems. Social engineering can be targeted – for example, the attacker might phone technical support, pretend to be a senior member of staff with a high level of access, and request that they change the password for the impersonated individual's user account so that the hackers can log in later. It is also employed in low-tech attack methods – a common tactic is to send out spam emails with virus-bearing attachments, which, when opened, log keystrokes or otherwise accumulate data (Trojans). 'Phishing' is a type of social engineering attack which many of us have encountered at some point – emails purporting to come from an authoritative source (such as a bank or credit card company) are sent out, requesting that the recipient enter their login details. The criminal can then gain access to their account to siphon off funds.

2. Denial of service (DOS)
   Attackers seek to overload a network with external communications requests to create a

server overload, preventing the target from performing its normal functions. The requests which make up the attack usually come from computers which have been infected with malware – without their owners even being aware of it. The Cyber Essentials scheme helps prevent your computer being used in such an attack.

3. Brute force
Attackers attempt to discover a password by using a program which tries all possible combinations of letters, numbers and punctuation marks. If the target is using a weak password, such as the name of a favourite football team or a dictionary word, this process is a relatively easy way to break into a system. It is also possible for some login systems to be fooled into giving up the password – if you have chosen to let your computer 'remember' it after you have logged out, then the attacker can use this against you.

4. Physical attack
Attackers steal data by gaining physical access to your systems. They use tactics which range from breaking into office buildings and stealing servers or laptops, to masquerading as employees to gain access during working hours so that they can install malware or infected hardware.

5. Exploiting vulnerabilities
Attackers gain access to systems using vulnerabilities that have been discovered in applications and configurations.

Cyber Essentials provides protection against the first three types of attack, which involve the use of malware – hostile or intrusive software.

It also helps you to repair vulnerabilities. Although it is not a requirement it may also be a good idea to make your office more physically secure as well – one sensible policy is to require staff to ask unfamiliar, unaccompanied visitors for identification, not just at reception but throughout the building.

The scope

The first step in becoming secure from such threats is to adequately scope which parts of your IT infrastructure need to be given a basic level of technical protection. This is defined firstly in terms of the business unit/ organisation and secondly in terms of the hardware and software used by that business unit, which will need to be made secure. The part of your IT infrastructure which stores and/or processes sensitive information will have to be included in the scope, but you can choose whether to have the rest of your organisation certified as well – this is an important decision to make up-front.

There is a helpful graphic in the *Requirements* which can be used to work out what is in scope, but the *Assurance Framework* goes into far greater detail on the subject and it is recommended that you consult that instead. This book examines scope in detail at the beginning of *Part 2*.

The five cyber security measures and implementing controls

The measures laid out in the *Requirements* have been chosen deliberately to protect against the low-tech attacks discussed above. Fully implementing these five key measures will put interlocking cyber security measures into place to defend your organisation.

The measures are:

1. Boundary firewalls and Internet gateways
2. Secure configuration
3. Access control
4. Malware protection
5. Patch management

After you have determined the scope, the next step is to implement the controls that make up each measure.

It should be noted that it is sometimes legitimately impossible to implement a control; the Cyber Essentials scheme recognises this and allows you to create compensating controls, which should be defined and put in place prior to the auditing process.

Documentation

Before you start implementing the controls, you should have established an approach to documenting your progress which can be used with all five measures. Documentation is important to ensure that the rules are being applied consistently across your organisation, and is required under the scheme in certain cases. It will also help you to fill out the self-assessment questionnaire when trying for Cyber Essentials certification.

Your suite of documentation should be based on the controls and explicitly linked to the network and user devices which are in scope for Cyber Essentials. It should be easily accessible to every member of staff who can make changes to these devices. Rules should be put in place to ensure that whenever staff work on these devices they must consult the documentation to find out the correct way to go about the changes, and must also make a note about what they have done; this will let you know that the rules/processes of the scheme have been correctly applied.

1. *Boundary firewalls and Internet gateways*

A boundary firewall is located at your organisation's Internet gateways (e.g. the modem, wireless router or dedicated gateway) rather than on your desktop PC or other device, and restricts connections to and from your entire network. This is the traditional place to put a firewall, although it is now becoming more common to also have additional firewalls on the other devices that make up the IT infrastructure ('host-based' firewalls). Restricting network traffic (by allowing only connections you have authorised) makes it far more difficult for attackers using commodity threats to gain unauthorised access via the Internet. Internet proxy servers and host-based Internet protection applications can also prevent your employees from accessing websites that will pass on a virus. The Cyber Essentials scheme therefore mandates that a boundary firewall or similar defensive apparatus must be put in place around the part of your IT infrastructure ruled to be 'in scope'.

There is a good chance that your organisation already has a firewall like this in place, especially if you are operating a small network with only one internet gateway, because most gateway devices will come with a firewall already installed. It is, however, necessary to take the following steps to make sure that it is providing the protection that it should.

Whether the firewall came installed with the product or you installed it yourself, you must ensure that the administrative password that came with the device is changed to an appropriately strong one (the default passwords may be generic or follow a specific pattern which hackers can discover and exploit). It is best to follow current guidelines about password strength.

Strong Passwords

There are a few widely accepted rules for creating a password that is difficult for an attacker to guess. A password:

- Should consist of eight or more characters and include a mix of lowercase letters, uppercase letters and numbers. Better still, include a symbol such as @, #, $ or %.

- Should not have been used recently or for another account – an online bank can probably safeguard your password, but if you have also used it for a less secure website then attackers can steal it from there and use it to gain access to your account.

- Should not be a dictionary word.

- Should not be the same as the associated username.

- Should not include information that an attacker could find from a social media account, e.g. the name of the user's favourite football team.

Alternatively, password management software may be a solution for larger organisations.

As well as ensuring the passwords are strong, there are other ways you need to configure the firewall. Above all, you must determine what connections the firewall will allow. Restricting network traffic involves setting rules to determine which connections are legitimate and which are not – both incoming and outgoing connections, to prevent hackers from easily moving data out of your organisation. Every rule that your organisation puts in place must be approved by an authorised individual – this must be documented, along with the reason that approval was given. Any services that are not approved, and those which are vulnerable to attack because they transmit unencrypted information (e.g. Server Message Block, NetBIOS, tftp, RPC, rlogin, rsh or rexec), must be disabled at the firewall by default.

Furthermore, any firewall rules that become obsolete must be removed or disabled.

Finally, there should be no external access from the Internet to the administrative interface used to manage the firewall configuration – if attackers can use it to disable or circumvent the boundary firewall, then they can move data into and out of your network far more easily.

If it should prove impossible to implement one or more of these controls, then alternative controls can be implemented. The *Requirements* gives the following example: if the firewall is being supported by an external services provider, then it is not practical to stop the interface from being connected to the Internet as they will have to access it remotely. Therefore strong additional security measures must be implemented (e.g. encrypting the connection, allowing only authorised individuals to access the interface, allowing only connections from whitelisted IP addresses).

2. Secure configuration

The aim in implementing this measure is to carry out a process called 'system hardening'. This consists of applying security controls which ensure that the devices and software which make up your IT infrastructure are properly configured to give maximum protection.

Correctly installing a device or a piece of software is about more than simply plugging it in. There are inherent risks in using some devices, simply because they are connected to the Internet, while other devices become a problem when they are not correctly installed or if default settings are not changed.

Default settings on computers and software can make a hacker's job easier, because unnecessary user accounts and unused applications that are left on your system are not as closely monitored. Applying the following controls will address these issues by ensuring your computers and network devices are set up for security.

All unnecessary accounts – both those created before purchase and those created for staff but no longer needed – must be removed or disabled to prevent them being misused by hackers. Your system is only as secure as the most vulnerable account, so if a default account has a weak password or is otherwise simple to break into then it is a threat to your entire IT Infrastructure – default account credentials are often freely available online or in manufacturer's documentation.

Similarly, all unnecessary software must be removed or disabled, including applications, system utilities and network services. Some software can provide hackers with access to sensitive information, while unremoved communications software (e.g. an instant messenger) could be hijacked to send data outside the company undetected.

Accounts that are in use must not be secured with a default password – and the new password should be strong, adhering to the principles laid down earlier.

The auto-run feature dictates what a system does when removable media are inserted – if it is enabled, the programs on a CD, memory stick or portable hard drive will start up automatically. Unfortunately, auto-run provides attackers with a way to get around employees' common sense– they probably know that they shouldn't open a suspicious email attachment, but will use a memory stick or CD without a second thought. Auto-run should be switched off to prevent programs from starting before somebody has taken a look at them and decided whether they are likely to be safe. This helps to prevent viruses from spreading between devices in your organisation, and also protects against social engineering attacks in which hackers leave removable storage devices in areas where they are likely to be found, hoping that an employee will be curious enough to look at them. Although it is not covered by Cyber Essentials, informing staff about the risks posed by unfamiliar programs is good practice.

A personal firewall, as distinct from the boundary firewall discussed above, must be installed on all desktop computers and laptops to provide an additional layer of protection. This helps to stop malware from spreading between the computers inside your security perimeter.

The fourth security measure in the Cyber Essentials scheme is the installation of anti-malware software. It is most effective to get both your personal firewall and anti-malware software from the same provider, as they often come as a package – doing so will ensure that they interact well and provide comprehensive protection.

It should be pointed out that creating your own standard configuration for network devices based on these controls is good business sense. It means that staff can more easily change devices, as they will already know where the relevant software is and won't have to deal with a strange interface. Furthermore, technical support will be able to easily implement common security controls, easily manage patches and vulnerabilities, and easily identify when a device is not functioning correctly. On the whole, a standard configuration will result in a more efficient operation. It is recommended that you base your standard configuration on those published by the National Institute of Standards and Technology (NIST) or the Centre for Internet Security (CIS).

3. User access control

Unnecessary user accounts are a risk because hackers may be able to take control of them. But even accounts which are in use and are therefore more closely monitored can be hijacked. Attackers can cause the most damage if they are able to gain access to an administrator's account or an account with special access privileges, because these privileged accounts have greater and more flexible access to information and systems. Business processes can be affected, information can be stolen or corrupted, and malware can be spread more easily to other parts of your network.

The following controls help to stop these sorts of attacks from succeeding, and are also intended to limit the damage when they do breach security. They follow the principle of 'least privilege' – i.e.,

accounts should only have access to information
and systems when it is absolutely necessary.

Each account which is created must go through an
established provisioning and approval process –
there should be no unused or unnecessary accounts
on your network. Administrative accounts should
be especially tightly controlled. Regarding special
access privileges, only those who actually need
them should be authorised to have them. You
should regularly review whether each employee
still needs their account or their privileges and
remove them as necessary. Details of who has
these special access privileges and why must be
documented and kept in a secure location – this
information could be very valuable to hackers as it
will tell them where to target attempts to penetrate
your organisation.

To prevent infection, administrative accounts
should not be connected to the Internet or email,
nor should they be used for everyday business
activities: their only purpose is to fulfil their
specialised administrative function.

It is also necessary to have a regimen of regular
password changes throughout your organisation,
as every time a password is used it is at risk of
compromise. As mentioned above, these
passwords should always be sufficiently strong
and each user should have their own account and
unique username. Before gaining access to
applications, computers and network devices a
user should have to enter their username and
password. This may seem obvious, but some kinds
of device used by many people in the organisation

and with access to sensitive information are often left without a system to verify the user's identity – good examples include fax machines and networked printers. When user accounts are no longer needed or have not been used for a pre-defined period, they must be removed or disabled. It is especially important that this rule is applied to administrative accounts.

4. Malware protection

The term malware (short for 'malicious software') covers any intrusive or hostile software.

Types of Malware

- A virus is a program that infects a device, copying itself from one file to another and one machine to another. Generally their purpose is sabotage – not to steal data but to render the device inoperable by deleting and corrupting files. Most viruses are attached to programs (executable files – .exe).

- Trojans (Trojan horses) have to be installed when the user runs a program, so are typically spread through social engineering (see above). They appear to be an innocuous application running in the background, but actually they are performing a sinister function such as setting up a backdoor which allows your device to be remotely controlled for sending out spam or performing a denial-of-service attack.

I: Requirements for Basic Technical Protection
from Cyber Attacks

- Computer worms automatically spread throughout your network using security holes.

- Scareware is a less common term, but this kind of attack may be familiar. It is malware which slows down your device while simultaneously purporting to be an antivirus program. Scareware performs a fake scan on your computer, claiming that it is infected with hundreds of viruses – then it demands that your pay a fee to remove them.

- Spyware is designed to collect information about you and send it to the attacker. By logging all of your keystrokes, for example, spyware can share your passwords with criminals.

- Adware (which showers you with popups) and 'free' programs are also part of the problem and will hurt the performance of your devices on top of their other negative effects.

- Ransomware restricts access to areas of the infected computer system until a ransom is paid to the hackers. It is an increasingly more common threat to businesses.

Malware protection, the fourth key measure of the scheme, is vitally important, as all devices which can connect to the Internet are at risk; fortunately, dedicated anti-malware software (also commonly called antivirus) is able to identify and disable the threats.

Cyber Essentials requires that such software is installed on all devices which are in scope and can be connected to the Internet. This includes desktop PCs, laptops, servers and mobile devices including any machines which are being used on a BYOD basis. Although not required, it is best practice to provide anti-malware protection even for devices which do not have any potential Internet access, because even though malware is mostly spread via the web it can also find its way onto your systems through removable media and can move between devices via your organisation's network connections.

When finding anti-malware for your organisation, it is best not to choose a free product. Any truly effective anti-malware, which gives a good level of protection and is regularly updated to deal with emerging threats, will cost money. Since you are also installing personal firewalls (as distinct from boundary firewalls) in line with the 'secure configuration' measure detailed above, it is a good idea to get an integrated package including both.

A further point is that running more than one firewall or multiple anti-malware suites on a device will significantly affect that device's performance and will actually make you less secure.

The controls for basic technical malware protection are quite straightforward. All desktops PCs, laptops and servers connected to the Internet must have some form of anti-malware software installed. Fortunately many devices come with anti-malware installed as standard. Note that **all devices which are capable of being connected** must be given the same protection; a device might not be connected right now, but an employee might plug it in one day without consulting anyone and without putting protection in place – so this stipulation ensures that everything will be secure now and in future. This anti-malware must be kept up to date – this can be done manually, but it is best to enable automatic updates to ensure that your devices are always protected from the latest threats.

The anti-malware software should be configured to regularly perform scans of all files (daily is best). It should also scan files automatically when the user attempts to access them, including when downloading or opening files – this covers not only files originating from the Internet, but also from removable media and from the company intranet. The anti-malware software also needs to scan websites when a user accesses them via a web browser such as Internet Explorer or Firefox.

It is a good idea to configure the anti-malware software to prevent users from disabling it, and to keep log files so that security professionals can look for weaknesses in the event of a breach.

Note that the anti-malware software also has to block access to websites which have been added to a blacklist due to the presence of malicious code; some malware protection software does this as a matter of course, some does not. Make sure the suite that you are purchasing offers this protection.

5. *Patch management*

This final key measure of the scheme is concerned with keeping your software up to date. Hackers are constantly innovating, finding new ways to break into existing systems and to exploit vulnerabilities. Although security professionals are equally untiring in their quest to stop cyber crime, they are unable to protect you if your systems are not receiving and installing the latest patches and fixes that they create. Some patches are of critical importance: in June 2009, for instance, 34 major corporations were hacked in 'Operation Aurora', a cyber attack launched by hackers affiliated with the People's Liberation Army of China, which exploited a previously unknown and unpatched vulnerability in Microsoft Internet Explorer. Attacks continued through February 2010, with target corporations including giants like Google, Northrop Grumman and Dow Chemica. This underlines the fact that no one can claim to be safe until a vulnerability is patched on their own network.

Vulnerabilities are commonplace in all kinds of popular software. Frequently they are the result of an oversight, especially if the program is a recent release – for example, a software developer leaves a backdoor in the security of the program he is working on to make his or a tester's job easier, but forgets to remove it at the end of the development process. Fortunately, software providers are aware of the risk to users and create patches to remove vulnerabilities as they are revealed. These patches are often released on a regular schedule, often once per week.

If you are running Windows it is particularly important to keep it patched – Microsoft's® operating systems and other popular programs (such as Outlook, or web browsers like Internet Explorer, Mozilla Firefox and Google Chrome) are very widely used, so a lot of malware and other commodity threats are designed to attack them specifically, and can proliferate quickly in the time between when a vulnerability is discovered and when it is patched.

The controls for this measure ensure that you are updating and patching your software in an organised fashion, making it less likely that hackers will damage your system by exploiting known vulnerabilities.

The first control is that any software installed on a device which can be connected to the Internet must be licensed and supported by the vendor or supplier. This should ensure that you will always have access to any patches that are released and that vulnerabilities are always addressed.

If the software you are using is very old, you may have to upgrade to a newer version in order to fulfil this requirement. This is because vendors eventually stop supporting out of date incarnations (for example, Microsoft stopped supporting Windows XP® from 8 April 2014). Users running unsupported software make a tempting target for hackers because any vulnerability they find is almost certainly unpatched, so any such software should also be completely removed from devices which can be connected to the Internet.

Just being supported is not enough – you also have to make sure that updates are installed rapidly after they are released. It is essential that new patches are always put into place within 30 days. It is best if they are installed immediately, though not necessary for the scheme. Security patches are, naturally, more important than other kinds of update. Installing these patches should be treated as a high priority – they should be put in place within 14 days of release.

To achieve this, it is often easier to allow updates to be installed automatically as soon as they are released by the vendor – many products are now configured to do this as a default setting. If this is your chosen method then it is still a good idea to occasionally check that updates are definitely being installed. Depending on your organisation, it might be better to make updates automatic rather than giving users the choice of whether to install them; we have all been guilty of putting off updates in order to save time, but it isn't a good idea.

PART II: ASSURANCE FRAMEWORK

Implementing the controls outlined in the *Requirements* is a valuable exercise for any organisation, but only by becoming certified can you show customers, investors, insurers and others that you are fully compliant.

Although the requirements of the scheme are relatively simple to meet, there is always a cost in time, money and organisational resources when applying a set of controls thoroughly and accurately across an organisation. Failing to pass the assurance process – falling at the final fence – will increase this cost, so it is sensible to be familiar with how the process will be carried out. This will improve your chance of succeeding first time.

To introduce you to how it works, we will first take a look at whether your organisation is ready to be certified and then move on to what the certification process for the Cyber Essentials scheme actually involves. Finally, we will examine the additional requirements for certification to Cyber Essentials Plus.

Scope

As mentioned earlier, the first step in implementing Cyber Essentials is to determine which parts of your IT infrastructure are in scope. This regulates what areas of your IT infrastructure you must apply the controls to. It also determines what the certificate (or 'mark') verifies as secure following a successful assessment.

You must clearly define the scope boundary around the part of your IT infrastructure used to handle sensitive data. This means working out who is managing this infrastructure (whether that is the organisation as a whole or a particular team/business unit); where is it physically located; and what is the boundary of the network.

Here are two helpful graphics to help you work out what you need to rule in scope for certification.

Figure 1 focuses on the organisation/business unit.

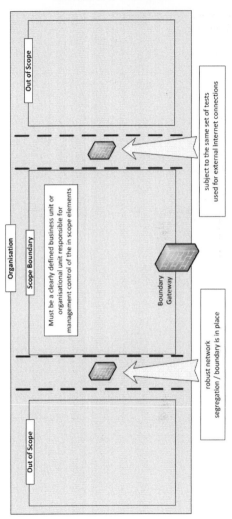

Figure 1: Organisation/business unit

Out of Scope

subject to the same set of tests used for external Internet connections

Organisation

Scope Boundary

Must be a clearly defined business unit or organisational unit responsible for management control of the in scope elements

Boundary Gateway

robust network segregation / boundary is in place

Out of Scope

Figure 2 covers software and hardware from a scoping perspective:

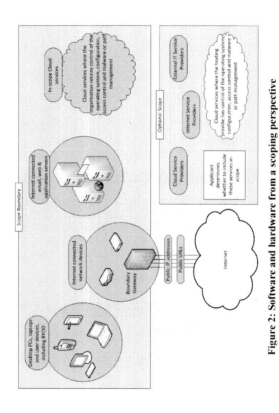

Figure 2: Software and hardware from a scoping perspective

The following hardware should be considered in scope:

- Desktop PCs
- Laptops
- Smartphones
- Tablets
- Wireless access points
- Email, web and application servers
- Devices used by employees to work from home and other machines used on a BYOD basis
- The boundary firewall and router

Note that mobile devices are also in scope, and if your organisation allows employees to use their own home computers or laptops, smartphones and tablets on a BYOD (bring your own device) basis these must be included in your security plans as well. You will need to apply all of the relevant controls to them.

It is just as important to protect devices used to work outside of the office as it is to protect your on-site hardware. In addition to the risk of theft or loss, these devices on the move may be exposed to threats when they are accessing open networks and can be mined for data by attackers. Worse still, if they are infected the virus can spread from them to other systems when they are connected to your office IT infrastructure. BYOD is a rapidly evolving area, and the UK Government will continue to monitor it and alter the *Assurance Framework* in line with developments.

Ensuring such BYOD devices are compliant poses a challenge, as employees have a greater degree of control over the hardware and software that they use. This can make it harder and perhaps more expensive to become compliant. A centralised approach is recommended – bringing in and checking all devices to make sure that security is consistently being upheld. Certification in this area should not, however, be too difficult because the assessors only have to look at devices representative of 90% of those used by an organisation, and because there is usually a standard application configuration for each device.

Note that you can purchase applications which will help to ensure that BYOD devices are operating in line with corporate requirements – e.g. they might maintain a separation between corporate and personal data to ensure a consistent level of security while maintaining the user's privacy. Boldon James, for example, offer a solution for mobile email that controls which messages can be synchronised to a device in order to ensure that sensitive data is not put at risk by loss, theft or malware.

Moving on, here is a list of areas outside the scope boundary:

- Users and privileged users
- Removable storage media
- Other business servers
- Bespoke systems

Users and privileged users are outside the scope, meaning that they do not have to be given training in cyber security for the organisation to become compliant. On the other hand, a basic level of awareness among staff regarding cyber security issues is highly recommended so that they do not accidentally undermine the controls you have put in place (by using weak passwords, for example).

If you are certifying only a sub-set of your IT infrastructure (for example, the systems used by a single business unit) then the same principles shown in the graphic apply. You must also make sure that the defences of this certified unit are not being undermined by connections to less secure systems in other parts of your organisation.

There are some special considerations when some of the IT infrastructure used by your company is not managed by your organisation but by other bodies including:

- External service providers (e.g. the hosting company for your website, remote technical support provider)
- Cloud providers
- Internet service providers (ISPs)

If external service providers are included in scope then you must be sure that the systems they are using to carry out business functions for you are appropriately secure. The easiest way is to find out whether the service provider is already certified either to Cyber Essentials or to a cyber security standard such as ISO27001 or the PCI DSS, in which case this can be used as adequate evidence that they have applied appropriate controls. If they are not certified, you will have to request details from them regarding their arrangements.

If you are seeking certification to Cyber Essentials Plus, you will have to go one step further: you must ensure that the IT infrastructure which is in scope, and that they are using to provide a service for you, is tested for compliance with the relevant controls. It is your responsibility to arrange permission for this.

Cloud services are increasingly popular, and providers in this area are something of a special case. If your organisation retains control of the operating system which is subject to cyber attack, and is responsible for configuring systems, controlling user access and installing patches, then you can implement the appropriate controls in each of these areas yourself and they will only be liable for controls relating to boundary firewalls. You will need permission to test from the cloud provider. If the cloud service provider performs these functions then it will be necessary to find out whether they are meeting the requirements of Cyber Essentials like any other external service provider.

When external service providers are not certified with other bodies, verifying that they are properly secure can be a challenge, but the Government considers it necessary with good reason; a system is only as secure as its weakest link.

Getting certified – are you ready?

When you have worked out and declared your scope, have implemented the controls and are confident that your organisation is now in line with all five key measures of the Cyber Essentials scheme, then you are ready to try for certification.

Here is a simple checklist to help you work out whether you are properly prepared – note that this is not a guarantee of readiness. It is possible to find a free, thorough, 'gap analysis' online which can tell you whether you are completely prepared.

To work out your score, add one point for each question that you answer with a 'yes'.

Control 1: Boundary firewalls and internet gateways

Question 1a: Do you have firewalls at all boundaries and gateways to your network?

Question 1b: Are your firewalls set to restrict inbound and outbound traffic to only authorised connections?

Question 1c: Are firewalls set to a default deny-all policy?

Control 2: Secure configuration

Question 2a: Do you have a configuration management system/process?

Question 2b: Does your standard device configuration include removal of all unnecessary software and user accounts?

Question 2c: Do you install personal firewalls on all mobile devices?

Control 3: User access control

Question 3a: Do you have a user account management system/process?

Question 3b: Are administrator accounts only used for administrator activities?

Control 4: Malware protection

Question 4a: Is malware protection installed on all devices that are capable of connecting to the Internet?

Question 4b: Does the malware solution automatically update?

Question 4c: Does the malware solution perform website blacklisting?

Control 5: Patch management

Question 5a: Is all software on Internet-connected devices licensed and supported by the vendor?

Question 5b: Are all vendor supplied patches installed in a timely manner (e.g. automatically)?

Question 5c: Are any devices running out-of-date (i.e., unsupported) software?

Results:

Add up your score and divide it by the total of 14 points in order to get your total 'readiness' score.

< 30%

A challenging road ahead:

Your organisation still has a long way to go to meet the requirements of Cyber Essentials. It's a good thing you checked before you got in touch with a certification body. You can now develop a plan of action to put these basic security controls in place.

30%–60%

You still have some work to do:

With this score you wouldn't pass the certification process. Your organisation has got some of the security controls in place, but you still have some work to do to become compliant. Depending on the security controls that are missing, you could still be open to a number of cyber attacks.

> 60%

You're Nearly There:

Your organisation has most of the security controls in place, and you haven't got far to go to potentially meet the requirements of the Cyber Essentials Scheme.

100%

This questionnaire is far from comprehensive, and should only be used after you have made a more thorough check. That said, if you scored 100% then you are likely to be able to get through the certification process.

Getting certified to Cyber Essentials

When you are ready to go ahead with certification then you must choose a certification body. Each of these organisations has been vetted by an accreditation body such as CREST or IASME, and each accreditation body has been appointed by the UK Government to ensure that they have the expertise to do so. Each certification body needs to have at least one member of staff with appropriate assessor's and quality assurance qualifications, who can measure organisations against the *Requirements*.

Choosing a certification body is quite straightforward. Companies which are members of CREST (a not-for-profit organisation that regulates the provision of professional technical services in the UK) or IASME are a good choice as they have been vetted to make sure they have appropriately competent employees. You can find a list of CREST accredited certifying bodies at *www.crest-approved.com*, or at their dedicated website *www.cyberessentials.org*. For IASME accredited certifying bodies, visit *www.iasme.co.uk/index.php/cyberessentialsprofile*.

Note that not every certification body will be able to cover Cyber Essentials Plus, so please do take this into account when making your decision – see below for further details.

The certification process for Cyber Essentials is equally simple. An appropriate person at your company will have to fill out the Cyber Essentials self-assessment questionnaire, which is supplied by your chosen certification body as the first step toward verifying your claim. After it has been completed a declaration must be signed stating that you are in compliance with the requirements of the scheme and that your responses to the questionnaire are accurate.

The signature must come from the business owner, the chief executive officer (CEO), somebody at board level or somebody in an equivalent role – without a signature from an appropriate person you will not be certified. If one person has both filled out the questionnaire and signed it, then it may be wise to ask another member of staff to review the document to verify that their conclusions are correct.

The Cyber Essentials questionnaire covers everything in the *Requirements*, and questions can be broken up into the following groups. Note that certification bodies can add further questions.

- Scope of Assessment
  o Organisation details
  o Remote Vulnerability Scan
  o Workstation Assessment
  o Cloud / Shared Services Assessment
- Security Controls
  o Boundary firewalls and Internet Gateways
  o Secure configuration
  o Access control
  o Malware protection
  o Patch Management

Fortunately, it isn't necessary to get every question 'right' – some are there simply to establish that your organisation is taking a broadly correct stance on cyber security. That said, some questions focus on aspects of security which are essential to get certification because they are direct requirements of Cyber Essentials. It is a good idea to take a look at the complete list.

After the questionnaire has been signed you can send it to the certification body, which will review it and decide whether your organisation has met the requirements of the Scheme. They will verify three things:

- that you have identified the scope to which is to be certified and that this scope is valid;

- that you have understood and complied with the requirements of the scheme;

- CREST-accredited certification bodies will run an external vulnerability scan focusing on external Internet-accessible systems, including dedicated hosting platforms. This scan does not form part of Cyber Essentials but is an additional service that CREST-accredited certification bodies can run.

Additionally, they will be able to let you know whether you have a reasonable prospect of passing Cyber Essentials Plus.

If they are satisfied after this verification process then they can award you the Cyber Essentials certificate or 'mark'.

If you are unhappy with the result handed down by the certification body, and feel that you have been unfairly denied a mark, then you can go to the accreditation body which authorised them – although it may be best to ask the certification body to reconsider matters first. The accreditation bodies are required to arbitrate between certification bodies and their clients regarding the results of the certification process.

Getting certified – Cyber Essentials Plus

Cyber Essentials Plus does not introduce any additional controls – it is more like a second more robust check that your IT infrastructure is secure.

This level of certification may give you the edge over competitors. Full compliance with the Cyber Essentials requirements is integral to this level of certification, and the only difference is at the test stage.

Certification bodies for this second stage are appointed by the accreditation body CREST. These companies must meet stringent requirements. The reason for the more careful selection of Cyber Essentials Plus certifying bodies is that, rather than having to simply verify the self-assessment process your organisation has performed, they must come to your office(s) and thoroughly check whether the solutions you have put in place comply with the control requirements. The requirements are designed to defend against the low-level technical threats and attacks outlined above.

This second stage is the acid test of your basic cyber security capabilities: the certification body will visit you to carry out an internal vulnerability test on your IT infrastructure, They will focus on workstations and mobile devices.

Their aim will be to find out whether the Cyber Essentials controls have been properly implemented and to check that known vulnerabilities have been addressed. They will check that individual controls have been implemented correctly and also simulate common cyber threats to see whether a hacking or phishing attack is likely to get through. This test of your preparedness will include all Internet gateways, and all servers providing services directly to unauthenticated Internet-based users within scope. For organisations using a BYOD model, it is important to note that they will also need to test user devices which are representative of 90% of the device types used in your operation.

If the certification body is satisfied that you meet the requirements of the scheme after this more thorough level of testing, they will then award you the Cyber Essentials Plus mark. The independent testing regime means that your customers can be even more certain that you are compliant with sensible cyber security rules and can protect their data from basic level threats.

As before, if you are unhappy with the results of your assessment you can approach the accreditation body for arbitration between your organisation and the certification body, although an appeal to your certifying body may be sufficient to have the decision reconsidered.

After the assessment

Note that you will have to be recertified annually to keep certain contracts or to continue bidding for them; it is possible that some customers and potential customers might insist that you do it even more frequently, although the UK government has not suggested this will be something they require as yet. This is because the assessment provides a 'snapshot' of your cyber security at a particular time and makes no statement about the continued viability of your approach. For example, it is possible that you will continue to make sure that new hardware and software is compliant with the scheme's requirements, but your organisation might not want the hassle and expense of monitoring devices used on a BYOD basis –

leaving a hole in your security which could lead to a data breach.

When your organisation has been certified and has perhaps won the desired contracts, it may be tempting to turn away from cyber security to focus on other business areas. It would be a mistake to let your cyber security slide, however, as there is a great deal of value in watchfully maintaining the security measures you have put in place.

The average organisational cost of a data breach in the UK has been consistently going up. According to the Department for Business, Industry and Skills' *Information Security Breaches Survey 2014* the cost has increased to £1.15 million for larger businesses, with 10% of respondents saying that their organisations were so badly affected that they had to change the nature of their business. Keeping up your basic cyber protection could quite literally save your organisation.

Staying on top of cyber security can also make a difference to bringing in new business and retaining existing customers. Organisations and customers are increasingly likely to check up on the security capabilities of their partners. If they ask to look at your arrangements it is best to be ready – it could mean the difference between gaining and losing a contract.

In the Overview of the scheme on page 3 of the *Assurance Framework,* it states that 'growing maturity' should be the goal for any organisation following certification. This means that the requirements of Cyber Essentials should become an integral part of your organisation's approach to information security risk management, and that as your organisation grows and becomes a more tempting target your attention to cyber security should grow with it – even to the point of implementing more robust arrangements such as those found in ISO27001 or the PCI DSS.

PART III: FURTHER ASSISTANCE

Practical help and consultancy

Although implementing Cyber Essentials is usually straightforward, it is understandable that some organisations will want help understanding what the controls mean for their organisation and to put them in place. Perhaps your organisation lacks technical expertise, perhaps it is very large, or perhaps you have to deal with a diverse and confusing IT infrastructure due to business processes, corporate mergers or other factors. It might be that you just don't want to use your internal resources when becoming compliant as your staff have productive work to do elsewhere.

If this is the case, bringing in outside assistance might be the right move. IT Governance is able to offer consulting services from experts in the field, helping your business to get certified more quickly and without undue hassle.

You can also consult the *CESG Listed Advisor Scheme* (CLAS) to find a reputable consultant as recommended by the UK Government. This scheme identifies appropriate individuals in the Information Assurance sector who can help to put the requirements of Cyber Essentials in place. The full list can be found at: *www.cesg.gov.uk.* On the other hand, non-CLAS consultants may be more qualified than those on the list, as CLAS was traditionally focused on those working exclusively in the public sector; it has only recently been broadened outside this area.

III: Further Assistance

Many private sector, non-CLAS, consultants may have better knowledge and skills regarding Cyber Essentials. As always, picking the right consultant can be difficult.

Useful documents and further information

There are a number of documents that expand upon the principles of Cyber Essentials. The *Requirements for basic technical protection from cyber attacks* identifies the UK Government's *10 Steps to Cyber Security: Executive Companion* as a source of useful information[1]. This was used as a source for creating the Cyber Essentials scheme, but it goes into greater detail about cyber threats and board responsibilities, as well as presenting real-world examples of damaging cyber attacks. Sharing this document around may be a good way to convince other board members of the need to act on cyber security or to continually monitor it following certification.

On the same webpage as *10 Steps to Cyber Security* you can find *Cyber risk management: a board level responsibility*. With a few well-chosen points, this document outlines why company directors need to take cyber security seriously. It also presents a selection of questions which professionals at board level can ask to help them quickly determine the readiness of their organisation to meet cyber threats. This is a useful tool for board members from a non-

---

[1] *www.gov.uk/government/publications/cyber-risk-management-a-board-level-responsibility.*

technical background. Meanwhile the *10 Steps to Cyber Security: Advice Sheets* provide more comprehensive general guidance on putting security measures in place, including both technical and organisational areas, although these guidelines do not offer the advantage of being part of a certification program.

For more information about the scheme, go to *www.cyberstreetwise.com/cyberessentials*.

The next step – cyber security standards

If you are looking to implement stronger protection, and also to reap the rewards of being certified to an internationally recognised standard, there are other options.

Cyber Essentials provides a basic level of protection, and this may be enough for some organisations. For larger or at-risk organisations, it may be a good idea to invest in better protection – especially if you are handling particularly sensitive data or are likely to face a more determined attack than the low-tech kind outlined in the introduction. For companies looking to take the next step in protecting their information and that of their customers, ISO/IEC 27001:2013 is a good choice.

ISO27001 gives you all the tools you need to create an information security management system (ISMS). As the recognised international standard for cyber security, it will also send a strong message to your customers and potential customers that you are taking their security seriously. Thanks to its recognition that good information security depends on people, processes and technology, it ensures appropriate technical and organisational measures are in place to combat cyber threats and is highly recommended by IT Governance. ISO27001 is supported by ISO/IEC 27002 which gives best practice, practical guidance on how to meet the controls.

When setting up an ISMS there are options other than ISO27001. The *Requirements* also recommends the Information Security Forum's *Standard of Good Practice for Information Security*. This covers even more topics than ISO27001, and it can be integrated with ISO/IEC 27002 and COBIT® 5.

Alternatively, the IASME Consortium have created their *Standard for Information Assurance for Small and Medium Sized Enterprises*. This does not have the same level of recognition enjoyed by the ISO standards, but it may be a good choice for smaller organisations as it has been written with their needs and capabilities in mind.

Implementing any of these standards will also ensure that you are compliant with the requirements of Cyber Essentials. Helpfully, Annex A of the *Requirements for basic technical protection from cyber attacks* lays out where the controls in this Scheme are present in the different standards – this allows companies which are in the process of putting the standards in place to check whether they are compliant with Cyber Essentials yet.

Staff training

Many people now recognise common cyber attacks when they see them and are aware that, for example, they should not open attachments from unsolicited emails. That said, it is a good idea to lay down some basic guidelines and to pass them on to your staff, ensuring that there is a consistent level of knowledge and good practice across your entire organisation. A truly effective security approach focuses on people as well as processes and technology.

The Cyber Essentials scheme already requires that all passwords, including those of ordinary network users, are sufficiently complex. Since you have to communicate this to staff anyway, this may be a good time to share other information.

In *10 Steps to Cyber Security* the UK Government suggests the following guidelines to set up a program for training staff:

- Produce a user security policy: Produce policies covering the acceptable and secure use of the organisation's systems.

- Establish a staff induction process: New users should receive training on their personal security responsibilities.

- Maintain user awareness of the threats: All users should receive regular refresher training on the cyber risks to the organisation.

- Support the formal assessment of Information Architecture skills: Encourage relevant staff to develop and formally validate their IA skills (i.e., the skills related to organising websites, the intranet, and software for usability and security).

Here are some suggested key outcomes for a cyber security training program. Staff should:

- be aware of their cyber security responsibilities

- use a strong password

- be on the lookout for attempts to trick them into divulging personal details or passwords

- know that they can be prosecuted for deliberately sharing passwords

- know not to send emails which could damage the company's reputation or jeopardise business

- be able to recognise typical 'phishing' emails

- know never to open spam under any circumstances.

Cyber resilience

Cyber security is your first line of defence but many experts now believe that with the proliferation of cyber attacks, one will inevitably get through the security measures of even the most well protected organisation. As a result, cyber resilience – defined as an organisation's ability to recover from a successful attack and return to business as usual – is being recognised as an important consideration.

Cyber resilience combines the disciplines of cyber security, incident response, business resilience, disaster recovery and even corporate communications. Putting a complex strategy like this in place requires a serious investment of time, resources and intellectual capital, so it is strongly recommended that you seek out expert guidance and dedicated cyber resilience resources before deciding whether to take this step.

ITG RESOURCES

IT Governance offers three unique solutions to help you meet the requirements of the Cyber Essentials scheme at a pace and for a budget that suits you.

As a CREST-accredited certification body, IT Governance can help you to achieve certification to either Cyber Essentials (CE) or Cyber Essentials Plus (CE Plus).

Do it yourself – solution

1. You read the requirements, implement them, then complete and submit the SAQ.
2. We then review the questionnaire, conduct an external scan for CE, and an internal scan and onsite assessment for CE Plus, and issue the certificate subject to compliance*.
3. Pricing
   a. Cyber Essentials – £400
   b. Cyber Essentials Plus – £1,150

Get a little help – solution

1. We teach you what to do, give you the tools, you implement, then complete and submit the SAQ.
2. We then review the questionnaire, conduct an external scan for CE, and an internal scan and

onsite assessment for CE Plus, and issue the certificate subject to compliance*.

3. Pricing
   a. Cyber Essentials – £885
   b. Cyber Essentials Plus – £1,635

Get a lot of help – solution

1. We come on site, show you what to do, and help you complete and submit the SAQ.

2. We then review the questionnaire, conduct an external scan for CE, and an internal scan and onsite assessment for CE Plus, and issue the certificate subject to compliance*.

3. Pricing
   a. Cyber Essentials – £1,245
   b. Cyber Essentials Plus – £1,995

* We will issue you with a certificate if you pass the scans and our technical assessor agrees that your questionnaire indicates compliance with the scheme requirements. The certification process is a different activity than the help and support activities we offer.

Conditions apply: The all-in fixed price solutions above are applicable to SMEs with approximately 250 staff, less than 16 IP addresses and based on one location only. Alternatively, contact us for a custom quote.

Visit *www.itgovernance.co.uk/ces-certification* for more information.